The Time

Breakthroughs in Mimetic Theory

Edited by William A. Johnsen

The Time Has Grown Short

René Girard, or the Last Law

Benoît Chantre

Translated by Trevor Cribben Merrill

Michigan State University Press

East Lansing

The first version of this essay appeared in 2010 in an edited volume, *René Girard: La théorie mimétique, de l'apprentissage à l'apocalypse* (Presses Universitaires de France). This version has been revised and expanded for publication as a separate volume.

♾ The paper used in this publication meets the minimum requirements of ANSI/NISO Z39.48-1992 (R 1997) (Permanence of Paper).

Michigan State University Press
East Lansing, Michigan 48823-5245

LIBRARY OF CONGRESS CATALOGING-IN-PUBLICATION DATA
Names: Chantre, Benoît, author. | Merrill, Trevor Cribben, translator.
Title: The time has grown short : René Girard, or the last law /
by Benoît Chantre ; translated by Trevor Cribben Merrill.
Other titles: *Clocher de Combray*. English
Description: East Lansing : Michigan State University Press, [2022] |
Series: Breakthroughs in mimetic theory | Originally published as "Le clocher de Combray: René Girard ou la dernière loi," in *René Girard: la théorie mimétique : de l'apprentissage à l'apocalypse* (Presses Universitaires de France). The first version of this essay appeared in 2010 in an edited volume, *René Girard: la théorie mimétique : de l'apprentissage à l'apocalypse* (Presses Universitaires de France). This version has been revised and expanded for publication as a separate volume. | Includes bibliographical references.
Identifiers: LCCN 2021039954 | ISBN 9781611864267 (paperback) | ISBN 9781609176952 (pdf) | ISBN 9781628954630 (epub) | ISBN 9781628964578 (kindle)
Subjects: LCSH: Girard, René, 1923–2015. | Bible. Romans — Criticism, interpretation, etc.
Classification: LCC B2430.G494 C42813 2022 | DDC 227/.106 — dc23
LC record available at https://lccn.loc.gov/2021039954

Cover and book design by Erin Kirk
Cover art © Ali Mazraie Shadi

Visit Michigan State University Press at *www.msupress.org*

Contents

Introduction

Faithful to both religious anthropology and the Judeo-Christian tradition, René Girard offers a synthesis
of archaic religion and an apology of Judeo-Christianity,
giving the old methods of typological analysis an original
twist. For Girard, it is no longer the biblical that prefigures
the Christian, but the archaic as a whole that prefigures
the messianic. This new typology, understood in light of
Girard's last book, *Battling to the End*,[1] proceeds by means
of three consecutive syntheses: a synthesis of archaic religion
(centered on the scapegoat mechanism and the institution
of sacrifice); a synthesis of messianic religion (prophetic and
Christian revelations dynamically rearticulated through a
demystification of sacrificial religions); and what Girard in
2007 called a "catholic synthesis,"[2] defined as a compossibiliy
of the first two and a resolution of their differences. Sacrifice

is turned against itself, in a *repetition* that exhausts its criminal and social dimension, so as to make visible its moral and personal dimension. Understood as a "sacrifice of sacrifice," the Judeo-Christian ethic is reaffirmed in a catholicity that is utterly Pauline in its inspiration, equally concerned with both ecumenism and a renewed dialogue with its Jewish source. Girard's approach is far from self-evident, and has elicited numerous misunderstandings. Some have judged it hasty, insufficiently grounded in its attempt to cover so many different disciplines. Be that as it may, Girard's insight has endured, and today we can measure its full strength. "Archaic," "biblical," "catholic"—such are the three syntheses accomplished in his oeuvre. The last of the three should not be understood in a purely denominational sense: Girardian catholicity, as we will see, is operational more than it is identitarian. It can be measured by its capacity for holding in tension two apparently contradictory religious modalities, and by its ability to derive important lessons from their compossibility.

We would fail to grasp the importance of this synthesis if we did not recognize the paradoxical source—both anthropological and theological—from which its strength derives. It is obvious, in light of the unceasing criticisms directed his way by both anthropologists and theologians, that Girard's approach was risky, and that it was bound to elicit a double ingratitude. The anthropologists reproached Girard for an overly intuitive comparativism, or for the fact that he hadn't found in the field the elements that he advanced in his theory. They forgot that Girard's theory is based on a morphogenetic mechanism seeking to hold for all human societies, and that as such it can appear only partially in any particular society. As for the theologians, they reproached Girard for the scientific pretentions of his defense of Christianity. The former, then, thought he wasn't scientific enough, while the latter thought he was too scientific . . . as if anthropology and theology could only exist by cutting their object in two, like King Solomon, depriving man of God and God of man. Girard wanted to keep these two sides together—indeed, the event of the Incarnation constitutes the central object of his meditation. The complex reception of his work is thus commensurate to the challenge that it poses—the challenge of connecting an anthropology of archaic religion with a Judeo-Christian theology. Such is the "anthropo-theology" (or "theo-anthropology") that Girard was calling for at the end of his career. I would like to respond to that call here by hazarding a mimetic interpretation of the Letter to the Romans.

I will deliberately emphasize the religious dimension of Girard's work. But I won't force anything on the texts. "Mimetic desire" is presented by Girard as a "deviated transcendence" that is unduly granted to the model whose proximity fascinates us; the scapegoat mechanism functions in the mimetic hypothesis as the generator of "self-transcendence," which comes from the group's capacity for exteriorizing its own violence in the form of the sacred; apocalyptic revelation, finally, is one and the same as the Pauline formulation of a "last law." Girard's "anthropo-theology" thus makes it possible to define and conceptualize an obedience commensurate with the growing enslavement experienced by humanity. This enslavement is caused by a denial of prophetic revelation. The new obedience implied by redemption is thus religious, as is the servitude of the subject caught in the skeins of mimetic desire: here we find the "closed"/"open" polarity established by Bergson in his 1932 *Two Sources of Morality and Religion*. Obedience to the "last law," which is a shift from one form of imitation to another, from the imitation of an exterior to that of an interior model, from "external" to "intimate" mediation (which, as we learn in *Battling to the End*, is not the same as "internal mediation"), assumes the gradual rise of messianic transcendence at the heart of world history. This ultimate transcendence ("authentic transcendence," Girard would say) and this ultimate model only appear "at the end." Prefigured by self-transcendence, they exceed and fulfill it. This is the origin of the Girardian oeuvre's fascinating and complex central thesis: it is in the disruption of ancient mechanisms for containing violence, in their essential exhaustion, that the true face of man and the true face of God conjointly appear.

I.

From Vertical Transcendence to Deviated Transcendence

Girard is a great reader of Proust. Starting in the 1950s, like François Mauriac at the same moment, he grasps the importance of *In Search of Lost Time* and gives it a central role in his first book, *Mensonge romantique et vérité romanesque* (1961) (*Deceit, Desire, and the Novel*). To introduce the key concepts of that book I would thus like to cite a passage from "Combray" (the first part of the first volume of Proust's novel) to which Girard accords tremendous significance. In chapter 9 of *Deceit, Desire, and the Novel*, "The Worlds of Proust," Girard evokes the irresistible nature of the "fall" that makes us ever more dependent on our models. This "descent into hell," which is a dive into worldly vanity, where the subject is more and more possessed by the other's desire—depriving him of "every authentic impression"—but which is also the sign of increasing enslavement within modern societies, is described as a growing distance with respect to a "mystical center." This point of reference is one of "vertical transcendence," which is gradually degraded into "deviated transcendence"—the attraction–repulsion felt toward a model who has become too close. Dostoevsky's oeuvre was the first to describe the ravages of this illusory transcendence.

In the world of Proust's narrator, this "center which is never reached, which is left further and further behind" is indicated by the steeple of Combray,[1] the village where the Narrator innocently admires his models (even if, Girard notes, "the Church is always empty" and "the human and earthly gods of external mediation have already become idols").[2] In the succeeding volumes of the *Search*, the Narrator distances himself from this point in concentric circles; external models become internal ones, ever closer and more fascinating. By contrast, Combray is the world where non-rivalrous admiration is still possible, a world where one still imitates models that are stable and provide structure, models close enough to the steeple to partake of its verticality. It is a childhood world where one *has faith in one's models*, where I am always open to learning from the other, and able to educate my freedom through contact with his. It is this "childish" faith of the Narrator that neutralizes the tendency of these models to become idols or obstacles to the fulfillment of his desires. "All the gods of Combray are assembled around this steeple," writes Girard, citing Proust:

> It was always to the steeple that one must return, always the steeple that dominated everything else, summoning the houses from an unexpected pinnacle, raised before me like the finger of God, whose body might have been concealed below among the crowd of humans without fear of my confusing it with them.[3]

Yet this ever-present possibility of "coming back" to the steeple as a reference point seems to contradict the later descent into the abysses of "metaphysical desire" (the shift from the world of Combray to that of the Verdurin salon), a descent Girard sees as obeying an ineluctable historical trend toward the rise of democratic egalitarianism already identified by Tocqueville and Stendhal at the dawn of the nineteenth century. In fact, this apparent contradiction aims at increasing our appreciation for the miracle of *Time Regained*. Only the final illumination of the party hosted by the Prince de Guermantes will be able to reverse this movement: the simultaneous experience of two separate moments of time, of "two fragments of duration," by a "pure Self" suddenly liberated from the slavery of desire and time, will assume the form of a mystical revelation, a return to the freshness of a world with which no competing vision (or aim) interferes. This "vertical" ecstasy is no mere dream nor does it resemble the myth of childhood recaptured: the child from the Combray period is ageless; he is already adult and potentially in thrall to the illusions of desire. He who recaptures his childhood manages this only after having wasted a great deal of time, at the end of a long and painful initiation. This revelation at the end of the Narrator's story naturally takes on apocalyptic overtones in Girard's reading. It's not so much the village of Combray as an Edenic universe that the Narrator connects with for a fleeting instant. Or rather he reaches the paradise of human relations only after having descended into the depths of an inferno of jealous reciprocity. This state of beatitude and communion only appears in Proust in the flash of memory, in a "fragment of time in the pure state" produced by the artwork's temporal synthesis.[4]

But we have not yet reached the stage of this "novelistic revelation." Girard is evoking the subject's growing alienation. The subject has left the universe where the idols were contained, kept at a distance *by the trust one had in them*, and is entering a world where this faith no longer exists, and where the idols have drawn closer, such that their desires become tangled up with those of the subject; this is the modern hell of "envy, jealousy, and impotent hatred," according to Stendhal, while in Proust it is the universe of the Verdurin couple, which is analyzed precisely in the same chapter 9 of *Deceit, Desire, and the Novel*: "The nearer the mediator comes to the desiring subject the more remote transcendency becomes from that vertical [the steeple]. It is deviated transcendency at work."[5] With the disintegration of cultural models (the descent from "external" to "internal mediation"), we move from constructive admiration to destructive rivalry. This *double degradation* (of model and subject), or this *loss of faith in the model*, is essential to an understanding of the mimetic insight. The closer the model comes to the subject, leaving its Olympian sphere to enter my own world, as if to avenge itself for no longer being admired—and this is necessarily the case in a democratic society swarming with models—the more I will have trouble not making my model into a rival. I will increasingly have a tendency to be jealous of him and to want to prove to him the precedence of my own desire, that is to say my capacity for becoming a model for this model. This is the stage that Girard calls "double mediation," where the jealous party in turn arouses his model's jealousy, and where the two rivals, clinging to their supposed differences, end up becoming identical: the asymmetrical relationship (of the subject oriented by his model) has become reciprocal; "triangular desire" (where the mediator dominates the subject) has become "mimetic desire" (where the subject is himself a mediator). The triangle has imploded: model *and object* have drawn closer to the desiring subject; the proximity of these three poles makes them tip into the "imaginary." Such are the dizzying metamorphoses of "metaphysical desire" analyzed by Girard.[6]

Yet Girard allows a rich ambiguity to hover over the pages where his central insight appears. This irreversible movement of descent can be interrupted by returns to "vertical transcendence"; the imploded triangle can recover its enlarged dimensions. Continuing to offer commentary on his citation from Proust, and suggesting the reversal produced by *Time Regained*, Girard evokes the "double movement of flight and return . . . prefigured in the evening pursuits of the crows of Saint-Hilary":

> From the tower windows, placed two by two, one pair above another . . . [the steeple] released, it let fall at regular intervals, flocks of jackdaws which would wheel noisily for a while, as though the ancient stones which allowed them to disport themselves without seeming to see them, becoming of a sudden untenantable and discharging some element of extreme perturbation, had struck them and driven them out.

Then, having crisscrossed in all directions the violet velvet of the evening air, they would return, suddenly calmed, to absorb themselves in the tower, baleful no longer but benignant.

The year is 1961. Girard has yet to describe the essential ambivalence of the scapegoat, who is both the one guilty of provoking disorder and the one who restores order; he would make this the subject of *Violence and the Sacred* in 1972. Yet it is very clear that the Proustian passage over which he lingers *preceded him* on the way to the later insight: the tower, a sign of vertical transcendence, finger of a god hidden in the crowd of humans—a god who is thus too human, but *pointing to* another transcendence, "baleful no longer but benignant." This single passage, like others taken from the *Search*, presages in a striking way the itinerary of Girard's insight, as if everything were there from the start. This "double movement of flight and return" lets it be understood that *the shift from one transcendence to another gives rhythm to human time: from order to panic, and from panic to order.* But—this is his rich ambiguity—over and against this circular temporality, which always rebuilds order out of disorder, Girard nevertheless continues to advance the idea of an irreversible movement that only a final revelation would be capable of stopping—a revelation prefigured, in *Deceit, Desire, and the Novel*, by the positive and quasi-religious "apocalypse" of *Time Regained*. Girard thus holds together two "untenable" universes: archaic religion, the universe of eternal return, and the messianic, the universe of a linear temporality giving onto the end of time; the "return of the gods" and the "return of God"; the ritual movement of return to order and the eschatological return of a divine that draws nearer in the wake of catastrophe. Such is the unfailing unity of the religious, whose nature Girard defines by affirming that the Bible reveals the centrality of the scapegoat mechanism. For the moment, let's hold on to the essential ambiguity of the transcendence highlighted here, a transcendence at once archaic and messianic: a divinity *sent forth by man* and a divinity *coming toward man*. It is on this tightrope that, for the time being, I would like my demonstration to remain balanced.

To conclude this first section, I would like to come back to the key concepts of what Girard, in *Deceit, Desire, and the Novel*, calls "the metaphysical structure of triangular desire." From Cervantes to Dostoevsky, the central thesis of this first book defines the progress of an "ontological sickness" of the modern world that can be measured thanks to the history of the novel, which is also a history of desire. The "metaphysical structure of desire," an essentially triangular structure (subject-mediator-object), whose variations ("double mediation," "masochism," "permanence in nothingness") indicate so many stages in a descending movement, *nonetheless remains triangular* through all its many metamorphoses. It's as if the smaller the triangle becomes, its three poles coming closer to one another, the more each of these three poles loses contact with the real. It is thus not only the object that loses its objective value to the competitive rivalry of the doubles; the subject and the model, because they mutually exchange roles, also lose all stability and become "imaginary" or "metaphysical." The structure of desire thus presupposes a double determinacy, on the part of the model and on that of the subject. The shift from "external mediation" to "internal mediation" measures the model's ever closer approach; the shift from admiration to rivalry measures the subject's growing slavery. However, although the "structure of triangular desire" is unique, these two movements are not necessarily linked, and can play out differently within the same framework. A father and a son, for example, if they seem by their very proximity to function in a regime of "internal mediation," still are not necessarily rivals. If the father's authority is respected by the son, the triangle of desire maintains its three poles at the right "spiritual distance," and the mediation can be qualified as "external."

But Don Quixote, for his part, although he seems to function in a regime of "external mediation" by imitating a far-off model sanctioned by his culture, is nonetheless the rival of Amadis of Gaul, whom he is trying to imitate: the triangle, which one might think was rather large, has begun to shrink, and the mediation is already in the process of becoming "internal." Thus Girard's insistence that "the opposition between *external* and *internal* mediation is not an opposition between Good and Evil, it is not an absolute separation." The "*folie douce*" of Quixote is still contained by culture: Quixote is, as Girard puts it, "an upside-down hero in a right-side up world."[7] But the degradation of values goes so fast in the modern period that Fabrice del Dongo, three centuries later, will owe his psychological salvation to nothing other than the passion that saves him: he is a "right-side-up hero in an upside-down world."[8] Psychological description and sociological description are mutually informative, but the social pathologies and the individual pathologies don't necessarily align: one can be crazy in a sane world and sane in a crazy one. In the first case, madness is contained by society; in the second, it is contained by the subject. Thus the "novelistic conversion" or the intelligence of the triangle of desire (which is an understanding of the right "spiritual distance" to maintain among the three poles) can make it possible to *hold on* in the midst of ongoing psychosocial breakdown.

We should be careful not to misconstrue the qualifiers "external" and "internal": the distance between model and object is not a spatial distance but a spiritual one. The model can be spatially close and spiritually external. This is the case of the father of a family when he doesn't enter into rivalry with his son; the faith of the son in his father, and that of the father in his son, maintains a healthy spiritual distance between them: the triangle is enlarged, the mediation is external. On the other hand, for there to be a conflict between father and son, the spiritual distance between the two must be reduced; *there must no longer be trust*. The son must be wary of the father, and the father wary of the son. Then the mediation becomes "internal."

Let's sum up as follows the variations of the "triangular desire" structure: the more the mediator is kept at the right spiritual distance *by the trust he inspires in me*, the more the risk of rivalry is likely to be contained; the more I am mistrustful of my mediator, on the other hand, the more he loses his spiritual distance (or my trust in him), the more the triangle tightens and the greater the risk of rivalry becomes. The crisis of the modern world is thus above all a loss of faith in the other. The rise of egalitarianism goes hand in hand with a loss of *credit*. Girard's second book, *Violence and the Sacred* (1972), will give this novelistic psychology a more distinctly sociological translation: class and caste distinctions, and the ritual differences that structure societies, are so many barriers against the rise of "undifferentiation." Should the confidence that structures them come to be shaken, these barriers will crumble: society will enter into crisis. And so it is the psychological and moral engine of institutions that Girard discovers in literature. There is an indissoluble link between trust and the social order, just as there is between distrust and disorder. The rise of distrust corrodes institutions. But this movement is irreversible. That's why the exacerbated crisis of the modern world calls for another type of trust, for—in Pauline terms—the irruption of faith at the heart of the Law.

It is indeed the "structure of desire" that will later make it possible for Girard to describe the religious structure itself. Desire is a triangle whose vertices are respectively occupied by a subject, a mediator, and an object; I never desire autonomously, but *more and more* by copying my desire from an other, and from an other who becomes *closer and closer* to me: there is a double movement of the model and of the subject. This evolution is essential to grasping the dynamism of the desiring structure. The object of desire has *less and less* an absolute value and *more and more* the merely relative value conferred upon it by the mediator. The modern world is thus characterized by the rise of competition that empties relationship of its content, gradually depriving individuals and the things they desire of their consistency: there is a loss of differences and the loss of a common world. The value of the object is relative to such an extent that, when the mediator and the subject enter into conflict, the object seems to have disappeared, as if we were now dealing with nothing but a couple of enemy brothers, each claiming over the other the priority of his own desire. Which shows that it's much less the object that is at stake here than the one who desires or could desire it. If I quickly prefer the dispute to the object of the dispute, that's because it's first of all the other who obsesses me, my mediator and his alleged autonomy, rather than the particular object of his desire. "Metaphysical desire" is desire of the alleged freedom that I perceive in the other. The more I mistrust the other, the more I envy him. It is the essence of the one who has become my rival—or his imaginary autonomy—that I idolize and seek to appropriate. Thus does "deviated transcendence" function: the loss of faith in the other is paradoxically a divinization of the other, who has become monstrous. This struggle for the appropriation of the other's freedom is much more violent than Hegel's struggle for recognition (which still assumes a possibility of mastery), but is nevertheless rooted in that struggle. Here it's not a question of "recognizing" the other but much more prosaically of stealing away his being.[9]

"Metaphysical desire" is thus an annihilation of the object, then of those who seek to appropriate it for themselves: envious mimesis is a logic of death.[10] It bears much less on the appropriation of an object than on that of an essence. The more the mediator and the object move closer to the subject (the more desire of the other becomes obsessive), the more reality itself will deteriorate, becoming imaginary. The quality of reality thus depends on that of relationship. A moral relationship ends up bringing into being a common world; a mimetic relationship fragments this world into simulacra, before making it disappear. That is why a mimetic relationship makes nothing come into being except rivals, who are fundamentally abstract beings, beings without consistency and all the more similar when they believe they are different. Nevertheless—and here one could speak of a form of Sartrean pessimism in Girard's approach—there is no possible extinction of the struggle. Thus the case of the coquette shows that indifference is the best strategy for defeating the other. But violence always ends up triumphing over the indifferent person, who only manages to exacerbate it: this is the case with the final suicide of Stavrogin in *The Possessed*. From Proustian snobbery to the Dostoevskian crime,[11] there is a difference not of nature but of degree: the distance between the mediator and the subject has merely been reduced, and with it the distance between admiration and rivalry. It's then that we leave behind instituted culture and descend into the violence of crowds, exchanging the "vertical transcendence" of civilization for the "deviated transcendence" of the collectivity. At this level of alienation, only a radical transcendence, Girard suggests, can come to save the subject. Grace becomes the final hope: the powerful conversion of Stepan Trofimovich at the end of *The Possessed*.

This call to grace (to the "novelistic conversion," a literary variant of religious conversion) is the proof that the back-and-forth from "deviated transcendence" to "vertical transcendence," such as that suggested by the movement of the crows in the steeple of Saint-Hilaire, is no longer functioning: the structure of metaphysical desire is temporalized, subject to aging. Although Girard at this stage has not yet defined the sacrificial mechanism that once made it possible to come back from the second transcendence to the first—from panic to order—he insists all the same on the unity of "triangular desire," even if there is "an immense spiritual gap" between the Amadis of Gaul of Don Quixote and the "models come down to earth" of Stendhal.[12] "Vertical transcendence" is measured by the spiritual distance between the mediator and the subject, that is to say, by the stability of trust; it is in some sense one with culture, and with aristocratic culture in particular. "Deviated transcendence" is measured by the jealous proximity between the mediator and the subject, by the rise of distrust: democratic culture, which multiplies possible models, also multiplies the risks of rivalry. It is easier and easier to hate, and less and less easy to admire. There follows, for the subject who is a victim of this imitation, a certain number of pathologies, which go from humiliation to murder or suicide, by way of masochism. But what can Don Quixote's "pleasant illusion"—that sweet madness where rivalry with the model has yet to make a dent in admiration—possibly have to do with the envious passion that Stendhal's Rênal and Valenod have for each other, this "double mediation" where the model has become a rival on both sides, where each has become a "model-obstacle" for his model? In other words, what ties can be established between the delights of "external mediation" and the modern hell of "double mediation"? Let's listen to Girard evoke the contagious nature of this final stage of imitation which makes the adversaries *identical*:

> But the connection clarifies precisely the metaphysical theory of desire and the inevitable transition from external to internal mediation. . . . All imitated desire, no matter how noble and inoffensive it appears at the beginning, gradually drags its victims down into the infernal regions. . . . From being double, reciprocal mediation could become triple, quadruple, multiple, until finally it affects the whole society.[13]

"All imitated desire . . . gradually drags its victims down into the infernal regions": the crisis of aristocratic models is irreversible. Everything leads to the conclusion that there is no way back from internal mediation. The only way out lies in a transformation internal to mediation itself—the "intimate mediation" evoked in *Battling to the End*, which is none other than grace, or the irruption, at the heart of a crisis, of "authentic" transcendence. This is where the jurisdiction of novelists ends. Novelists are skillful at spotting all the metamorphoses of the triangle of desire, but within the psychological and sociological frameworks of an individual in crisis and a culture coming apart at the seams. And here begins a new stage in the Girardian analysis. Let's bear in mind the following two movements, the first real and irreversible, the second hypothetical: *when external mediation collapses into internal mediation and admiration crumbles into rivalry, differences are reduced; if internal mediation relaxed into external mediation and a restored distance made the discernment of good models possible once more, differences would reappear and the risks of rivalry would be reduced.* In reality this is not what happens: the "return of confidence," as is said in economics, is no longer possible, except in another manner—what René Girard calls "novelistic conversion," in which for a brief instant the individual leaves the mirages of desire and time behind—an experience that is nonetheless strong enough to transform the novelist's life. And yet these moments of grace don't seem able to counter what Girard describes as an inescapable rise of slavery, which conversely is also a descent into the abysses of "metaphysical desire" and an ever-growing distrust. In this desire that "increases on both sides at once," what we witness is a mutual alienation: the other is alienated to myself, and I am myself alienated to myself; or else I am alienated to the other, and the other is alienated to himself. What mimetic desire causes to disappear in this tightening of the triangular structure is the irreducible difference of each of us; what it causes to appear is the point toward which it aims: undifferentiation. To the extent that metaphysical desire deteriorates relations among men, I become little by little an idol for the other and an idol for myself. This "escalation to extremes" of desire is nothing other than what Girard, in *Violence and the Sacred*, calls "essential violence," the only transcendence that we are able to produce now that the return of "vertical transcendence" seems to be compromised once and for all. *Unless, that is, vertical transcendence has changed its nature, unless a decisive event has modified the structure of religion itself.* That's how we can explain that the world still *holds together*, Girard suggests. But in 1961 Girard can do no more than imply that which he still lacks the means of affirming. For the moment, let's say that the progress of "metaphysical desire," an irreversible regression, calls more and more for another transcendence.

Girard offers ways to think through the movement of history as a growing servitude of individuals more and more enslaved by their desire. But the growing inability to come back to "vertical transcendence" and the rise of distrust produced by this impotence are mysteriously made up for by an increasing proximity with regard to another transcendence, a horizontal or messianic transcendence that *comes to man in the wake of catastrophe*. The rise of slavery is thus the negative side of a return of the divine, of an essential *parousia*, which is the return *of the only* and *to the only* possible model according to Girard: the Christian model, which is becoming more and more present, he says, echoing Max Scheler's analyses in *Ressentiment*.[14] But Christian mediation, which Girard will later define as an imitation of the "consenting scapegoat"—the imitation of a paradoxical model, who erased himself as obstacle, an invisible model or one who leads us beyond the visible—has not yet emerged in his reflection. If the return to "vertical transcendence" proves more and more impossible, even as the "ontological sickness" advances, the imminence of catastrophe itself shows that the distance from human beings to the divine is being reduced: the *growing proximity* of good transcendence is the eschatological inverse of the *increasing promiscuity* of "deviated transcendence." It is at the height of the mimetic crisis that the spectacular conversions in Dostoevsky's novels take place—a proof that the true God moves in the wake of evil, or that the Messiah makes use of the Devil. Such is the paradoxical inscription of Christianity in history that it realizes itself in its very failure. *The return to "positive transcendence" is accomplished, one might say, less and less in a vertical dimension and more and more in a horizontal one*: according to Girard, this is the decisive shift that Christian revelation has operated on religious structure and, as a result, on time and history. So do the jackdaws come and go around the steeple of Combray. So varies, but always in a certain direction, the one triangle of desire, becoming narrower and narrower, less and less capable of recovering the good spiritual distance between its three poles. In his first book, Girard seems to assume that only the first movement takes place, in an irreversible manner. In the opposite movement, which he recognizes thanks to the miracle of "time regained"—a discreet but clear allusion to his own return to Christian faith, which has something of both novelistic and religious conversion about it—he is just beginning to glimpse the *trace* of a much more fundamental mechanism, the very one that gave birth to culture.

II.

Self-Transcendence, the Scapegoat Mechanism, and the Institution of Sacrifice

I have deliberately emphasized the terminological slippage in Girard's central concept: at its ultimate stage "triangular desire" becomes "double mediation," and the triangle tightens until it is indistinguishable from that point of identity and undifferentiation. The first book stops here as if before a limit that cannot be exceeded. The frequency of the theme of enemy brothers in mythology and tragedy will enable Girard to switch to a new playing field, to move from literature to religion *stricto sensu*: to go from the attentive reading of Greek tragedians to a revolutionary analysis of rites and taboos. This new investigation is the subject of his second book, *Violence and the Sacred*, published in 1972. Its result is the emergence of the second "pillar" of the mimetic theory: the scapegoat mechanism, the morphogenetic principle at the origin of all human societies, capable of explaining what made possible the shift from panic to order, from the collectivity to civilization. This mechanism, whose trace or avatars Girard spotted in the tightening and loosening of triangular desire and the play of external and internal mediation, would become the key of his anthropological system.

As Lucien Scubla has shown,[1] this second book offers an audacious synthesis of numerous insights that preceded it: from English anthropology (Frazer, Robertson-Smith, Malinowski, Hocart) to Freud, by way of French anthropology (Durkheim, Hubert and Mauss), Girard's discovery makes it possible to gather numerous scattered elements (the primacy of rite over myth, the idea of sacrifice as an operation that distances the sacred, the social definition of religion, the idea of an original lynching, the unity of rites with kingship at the center), such that all of these facts can henceforth be understood as orbiting around the founding murder. Thus "mimetic desire," understood as the contagious deterioration of social ties and the driving force of the disintegration of Western values, is the trace within culture of a much more profound drama—what Girard now calls "undifferentiation" or "sacrificial crisis," corresponding to a confusion of legal and illegal violence. This catastrophe, which is supposed to have taken place at the origin of the first human societies, always comes back and increasingly does so as *the* threat to be warded off. Although the first human groups may have disappeared due to the effects of internal violence, the "sacrificial crisis" is nevertheless described within a framework indicated *a posteriori* by the solution proper to ritual: the crisis precedes the focus of all individuals on one scapegoat victim, through whom order is restored to the group. The scapegoat mechanism is thus that which undergirds the institution of sacrifice. It comes after the possible implosion of the first human societies; it is intermediate between chaos and order. This collective lynching is repeated each time a society experiences a crisis that its (religious or political) rituals are unable to contain. As a mechanism, the founding murder is not, in Girard's mind, a mere concept that makes it possible to "hold together" complementary elements; it is also much more than a synthesis corroborating and unifying scattered insights. It constitutes a *real event*, which the imaginary of myth always masks. On this point, the unambiguous conclusion of the book deserves a hearing:

> My theory depends on a number of basic premises. Even if innumerable intermediary stages exist between the spontaneous outburst of violence and its religious imitations, even if it is only these imitations that come to our notice, I want to stress that these imitations had their origin in a real event. The actuality of this event, over and above its existence in rite and record, must be kept in mind. We must also take care not to restrict this event to any one context, any one dominant intellectual framework, whether semantic or symbolic, which lacks a firm basis in reality. The event should be viewed as an absolute beginning, signifying the passage from nonhuman to human, as well as a relative beginning for the societies in question.[2]

Thus sacrificial ritual is defined as an *imitation* of the spontaneous violence that always threatens to return. It replays in an infinitely varied fashion ("innumerable intermediatory stages") a founding (and refounding) mechanism, the one whose universality was shown by the unity of triangular desire. This event can be deduced starting from mimetic desire: it is toward this discovery that Girard is moving in his first book, when he glimpses the essentially contagious nature of "reciprocal mediation": "From being double, reciprocal mediation could become triple, quadruple, multiple, until finally it affects the whole society." All human societies bear in themselves the trace of the trauma over and against which they were constituted, namely the contagious loss of all differences, signifying the pure and simple extinction of these societies. Rites are a much more faithful echo of this trauma than are myths: from the sacrifice of twins, described by ethnologists in primitive societies, to the *mundus inversus* of cathartic dances and rites, it is always the same sacrificial crisis, the same loss of differences to which a preventive remedy must be applied. This crisis—*mimed* by ritual and *avoided* by taboos and prohibitions, thus structuring the whole edifice of the religious—is the state of fusion of a group that has been undifferentiated by the rivalries that devour it, a social body fragmented into thousands of couples of enemy brothers.

It suffices to take a look at what rituals do (and at what myths hide, since the mechanism can only function if it is concealed), and the thread of all human institutions is unspooled, to the point where the crisis for which the scapegoat mechanism offers a remedy can be glimpsed: on the verge of implosion, the group turns suddenly against a victim chosen at random by a blind and spontaneous process of convergence, and directs all of its violence against that victim. This victim *must* be held responsible for the disorder; its guilt *must* be established—a guilt that is, no doubt, confused and social, but that is nonetheless guilt. The group is then gripped by a collective fascination for this individual chosen at random because of a very slight difference, which eventually becomes a monstrous difference as a result of the contagion of desire—which goes to show that what is at stake is not individual guilt but a collective hallucination. This is why the scapegoat mechanism which comes back whenever rituals lose their efficiency will be ritually imitated, indefinitely repeated, with preventive ends in view and in a more and more meticulous fashion. The extraordinary magico-ritual precision of Vedic India, which Girard addressed in 2003 in a series of three lectures in homage to Sylvain Lévi,[3] in itself calls for a "ritology" or a scientific study of rituals despite the fact that the appeal of structuralism overshadowed this fledgling science at the dawn of the twentieth century. Thus the preventive remedy *imitates* the curative one, the sacrificial victim *repeats* the scapegoat: it is this *repetition* that ends up structuring the whole archaic religious edifice and, more broadly, the totality of human societies. It is a vital repetition that works against monotony, decrepitude, and the lethal forgetting of traditions.

And so the enslavement of the subject kneeling at the feet of its mediator in *Deceit, Desire, and the Novel* has in *Violence and the Sacred* become the fascination of a whole group for a single Rival, a single Model-Obstacle, responsible for all evils and, once immolated, divine restorer of the threatened order. The process of self-divinization (I alienate myself to the other because this other is alienated to himself, and vice versa) takes on a social dimension in Girard's second book: it is the whole group which, through a global mechanism of convergence,[4] is fascinated by its future victim, alienates itself to that victim, *worships itself through that victim*. This victim who is "responsible for all evils" is fascinating in its very malignity, but also in its power, for calm returns thanks to its immolation. The individual crisis of mimetic desire has become collective, but it is triggered by the same causes, such that Girard will sometimes refer to the strategies of the coquette to attempt to understand the passivity of the victim who is himself carried away by the contagious spiral of violence. It is thus because it extends the *deceptive* logic visible in triangular desire to all of mythology, because it shows the mimetic relationship to be that which both causes and threatens social order, that Girard discovers the principle of the sacred in all human societies: religion is in the first place a management of violence, the ruse that enables human societies not to destroy themselves.

And so Girard's theory quickly emerges as "the first atheistic theory of religion."[5] It supposes that all gods were first victims of the scapegoat mechanism, which is shown in myths by the traces of stereotypes of persecution that some of them display (gods who are one-eyed, lame, sick, foreign . . .). The refinement of this mechanism, its perfecting or progress effected by the repetition of ritual, made possible both the development of religion and that of the cognitive capacities of the first humans. But this transformation of "all against all" (generalized mimetic rivalry) into "all against one" (the scapegoat mechanism) cannot be a deliberate process: the misrecognition proper to those who *are acted upon* by the scapegoat mechanism testifies to the fact that we are dealing with a phenomenon of social physics, or an immanent resolution of the crisis. This phenomenon will in turn be *repeated* in ritual misrecognition (a more developed misrecognition, which should be qualified as "second-order"). This mimetic re-elaboration of lynching through ritual, this repetition (or deepening) of the scapegoat mechanism, is already progress in awareness, even if this awareness remains obscure. This point is essential: ritual is a "distorted" awareness, *but it is not a lie*, unlike myth which, Girard demonstrates, will always try to make the traces of the collective murder disappear so as to complete the divinity production process.

Armed with this reconstruction of the primal scene, Girard—following Freud's insight into originary lynching, but substituting a mechanism capable of acting anywhere and everywhere for a singular prehistoric event—sets out to describe the genesis of institutions and thus of culture. The ritual repetition of the scapegoat mechanism, substituting a *sacrificial* victim for a *scapegoat* victim, is what enabled humanity to detach itself gradually from animality: man becomes a "symbolic animal."[6] Increasingly complex rites and prohibitions will be better and better able to ward off the return of crisis, thus making possible institutions and culture in general. And so it is primitive lynching and its ritual repetition—the scapegoat mechanism and the institution of sacrifice—that made possible the emergence of humanity. Girard offers both an "absolute origin" of man and a "relative origin" of particular human societies; in other words, a morphogenetic principle based on the misrecognition of individuals who literally "do not know what they are doing" but who, in an immanent fashion, which is to say *without being aware of it*, keep recreating order from disorder, culture out of chaos. The resolution of the crisis at the expense of a scapegoat is not the group's conscious decision. The misrecognition peculiar to lynching and the more developed misrecognition of ritual sacrifice are fundamental for Girardian theory, for it is these two levels of misrecognition, these two substitutions, which alone make ritual effective.

The back-and-forth from "deviated transcendence" to "vertical transcendence" has become in *Violence and the Sacred* a shift from order to panic and from panic to order. But this mechanism of self-transcendence (or of exteriorization of violence in the form of the sacred) has gradually "seized up," as if over the course of millennia it had exhausted its rich possibilities. The primarily *curative* efficiency of lynching and the primarily *preventive* efficiency of ritual are thus revealed by the traces the connection between them has left in culture. In fact, the play of external and internal mediations in modern civilization is but one of the avatars of sacrifice, which always remakes order out of disorder. Sacrifice is addressed to gods made by men, as the disintegration of institutions and the exacerbation of "metaphysical desire" from Quixote to Stavrogin makes it possible for us to see today. Inasmuch as they are witnesses of the degradation of human relations, the great novelists have had the privilege of going behind the scenes: the "abysses of desire" are as precious a source of information as certain mythological themes about originary chaos, from whose undifferentiated depths issued the structuring differences of culture. The fact that these differences are once again being erased lets us see that *the structure has been affected in an irreversible way, yet without ceasing to be the same.* That is why from the very beginning Girard sees eschatology as the form of rationality capable of accounting for the new configuration of the religious: the return of good transcendence will continue to function, he suggests in the concluding sections of *Violence and the Sacred*, but in another manner. The English and French anthropologists of the late nineteenth and early twentieth centuries were both right and wrong: the Judeo-Christian religion is indeed a form of religion like any other, and yet in its very *repetition* of religious structure it inscribes a decisive *difference*—a difference that will make everything comprehensible, that will reveal everything, Girard suggests.

The efficiency of rituals is only possible if misrecognition continues to function after the founding murder. This is one of the fundamental points of Girard's theory. But over time this misrecognition deepens and is interiorized. The more human beings master their rituals, the better they understand them, the more these rituals tend to become confused with the responsibility that falls to each individual. The ability to describe the scapegoat mechanism proves that we have come out of a certain type of collective hallucination, that we have ceased to believe that the victim is guilty, that *a repetition of a new kind* has been inscribed in history, deepening the misrecognition of ritual and constituting a new step in our insight into the founding murder. Such is the unsettling light that illuminates the end of *Violence and the Sacred*:

> That ethnology is alive today, when the traditional modes of interpretation are sick unto death, is evidence of a new sacrificial crisis. This crisis is similar but not identical to previous ones. We have managed to extricate ourselves from the sacred somewhat more successfully than other societies have done, to the point of losing all memory of generative violence; but we are now about to rediscover it. The essential violence returns to us in a spectacular manner—not only in the form of a violent history but also in the

form of subversive knowledge. This crisis invites us, for the very first time, to violate the taboo that neither Heraclitus nor Euripides could ever quite manage to violate, and to expose to the light of reason the role played by violence in human society.[7]

"This crisis is similar but not identical to previous ones": there is no turning back from the decomposition of archaic religion; the ritual containment of violence loses its efficiency. But then how does the world hold together under the nuclear threat? Girard never stopped being amazed at this, ascribing this veritable miracle to a transformation of religion. In *Violence and the Sacred*, archaic religion is implicitly defined (Girard's readers will discover this afterwards, in *Things Hidden since the Foundation of the World*) as a "figure" of messianic religion. And the latter mysteriously goes hand in hand with the degradation of values that characterizes the modern period. The crisis of the modern world is a prelude to the return of a transcendence that is *other*. This amounts to saying that *parousia*—the growing "presence" in history of this other transcendence—is made intelligible in a new way by the mimetic theory that Girard was then in the process of constructing. The promise Girard makes to his readers as he finishes his second book is an eschatological one: he tells us that we are going to witness a return of "essential" and "spectacular" violence. The mere fact of being able to understand the scapegoat mechanism, thanks to the contributions of ethnology, is the surest symptom that we have entered a new era. Self-transcendence, the immanent production of the sacred, *was thus gesturing at another transcendence*: messianic transcendence, whose growing presence is inscribed at the heart of "essential violence." Recall the steeple of Combray seen by the narrator of the *Search* "raised before me like the finger of God, whose body might have been concealed below among the crowd of humans without fear of my confusing it with them." Religion is only *partly* immersed "in the crowd of humans"; Proust's great contemporary Durkheim was only *partly* right. There is no self-transcendence without transcendence. Girard's second book makes its way toward a third stage: by deepening our understanding of ritual and the origin of all rites, Judeo-Christian prophecy liberates humanity from its subjection to sacrificial religion. But since the human *structure* is religious, and given the degree to which violence threatens the world once it is chased from its hiding place, this revelation (the latest twist in that structure) *subjects us for that very reason to a still more onerous law.*

Why speak so urgently of danger? This is a fundamental point which accounts for the universalization of the threat. The violence uncovered by the revelation of the innocence of all scapegoats (or by the appearance of a third type of victim, the innocent victim of the Bible who comes after the *ritual* victim and the *scapegoat* victim) is now deprived of its outlet and will escalate to extremes. What is the engine driving this universalization of violence? The invention of the modern state, that Leviathan which ends up being the only solution to human violence. Bearing witness to an undeniable progress in mastering violence, but only within given territories and in ever greater opposition to their neighbors,[8] modern political institutions have increased that violence to the point of globalizing it with the nuclear threat. There was a great deal of lucidity in misrecognition and its ritual developments, and Girard repeatedly suggests that there is a great deal of misrecognition in juridico-political lucidity.

Indeed, the state apparatus takes over with enviable efficiency for sacrificial institutions. It reveals itself to be capable of striking at the heart of violence without fear of retaliation. But this monopoly on legitimate violence has exacerbated misrecognition. The invention of the state comes in the wake of the breakdown of archaic ritual; it bears witness to an aggravated loss of faith in ritual. The political dominates the scapegoat mechanism from the outside but proves unable to interiorize it. So the increasing enslavement of humanity goes hand in hand with the advent of the state. In established nations, the alienation of each one of us to the threatening other accompanies a gradual disappearance of ancient rules of solidarity. This change leads to an atomization of individuals: undifferentiation has become indifference. The state can then act with total impunity, as was demonstrated by the genocides of the twentieth century.

According to Girard, it is this modern servitude that the prophets anticipated. The prophets emphasized the obedience necessary to maintain the religious structure without making it explode, and with it the very idea of humanity. This obedience is nothing other than faith in the innocence of the Suffering Servant of Isaiah, made definitively new in the Passion of Christ. Thus we can understand the profundity of Girard's insight: the fatigue of the sacrificial system, its very agedness, is part of a *loss of faith in ritual*. It could be said that the modern state is born of this loss of faith and that the state has been considerably strengthened by its rejection of the prophetic. The Passion of Christ closes the prophetic sequence and heralds the advent of state reason. The declaration of Caiaphas precedes Pilate's decision: "it is expedient for you that one man should die for the people, and that the whole nation should not perish."[9] Something essential for the future of humanity is expressed in this closing of the messianic moment, which the emergence of modern politics has gradually silenced. After the exhaustion of a certain tendency of ritual, there came another, prophetic tendency *that deepened the intelligence of the Law, and also of sacrifice, but did not reject it*. This other tendency, a new *repetition* and a new *deepening* of the religious structure, has been deliberately misunderstood by the political order, which has even constituted itself against that tendency. As Girard writes *Violence and the Sacred* and meditates on the lesson of the Greek tragedians, he lets it be understood that his next book will be devoted to biblical prophecy.[10] By making the innocent victim appear, prophecy bears witness to a final twist imposed on the religious structure. *Just as the sacrificial victim repeats the scapegoat victim, the innocent victim of the Bible repeats the sacrificial victim.* This second repetition *exceeds* the religious structure: it brings it literally beyond itself. And so it is very natural that Girard's second book should open up onto a third book devoted to Christianity.[11]

III.
Messianic Transcendence

If Girard often notes that the analyses of religion in *Violence and the Sacred* only concern its archaic modality, this is because a historical event took place that, according to him, was as decisive as the invention of sacrifice in prehistorical times. This event, this decisive repetition of the religious structure, which introduced a profound dysfunction into the matrix of gods, rules, and laws, is the Passion of Christ, which was foretold by the Jewish prophetic tradition and, as Simone Weil wrote, intervened "at a point in space, in a moment in time." This event, which according to Girard is irreversible, attests to a fundamental change of the sacrificial mechanism and of all rites and institutions, which ever since have only been able to *delay* their own disintegration. This is the thesis of *Things Hidden since the Foundation of the World*,[1] published in 1978—the demystification of the archaic by the revelation on Golgotha of the secret basis of all human institutions. Such a powerful statement paradoxically did a disservice to Girard's thesis: by summarizing his central insight too quickly, the book's "spectacular" quality tended to smother the systematic nature of the approach that made it possible. But we should take this insight with the greatest seriousness. Girard's insight pushes to its logical endpoint the idea of the back-and-forth movement from "deviated transcendence" to "vertical transcendence," putting the latter into the horizontal historical perspective of Saint Paul's "the time has grown short," which expresses the urgency of the messianic. Let's try to formulate the radicality of Girard's insight: *there will only be a "return" to true transcendence in an extenuation of history, which has literally been driven mad by the revelation of its sacrificial engine.* This authentic transcendence, which is not man-made, is not granted immediately (this would be to fall back into the Marcionist impasse).[2] It must coincide with the *eschaton*, the moment when historical time, according to Saint Paul, implodes into eternity.

Here Girard connects his thought with both religious anthropology and with what that anthropology tried to erase: the messianic or Judeo-Christian *difference*. Supposing that original sin, which Pascal found scandalous—although he recognized that without it "man would be even more incomprehensible to himself"—was the same thing as mimetic desire and the scapegoat mechanism? Girard's hypothesis puts less emphasis on the moral dimension of the prevarication than on the *unfinished character* of primitive religion: Revelation accelerates the process of hominization—a process of which mimetic desire is the engine—to the point of letting mankind glimpse a possible exit from its specific limits. Thus Revelation "finishes off" humanity, with all the terrible ambivalence of this verb. The revealed innocence of Christ, while washing all scapegoats of their social guilt, which is the mystification necessary to the working of the scapegoat mechanism, attests to the fact that the old return to vertical transcendence can no longer function. It causes the advent of a completely different type of transcendence— the transcendence of *parousia*, the growing "presence" of another transcendence, which this time is at the heart of human history. This is as much to say that it opens onto the apocalyptic dimension of that history. For Christ puts humanity before the terrible choice between accepting the

Kingdom and renouncing violence or destroying itself by letting that violence "escalate to extremes."

It is obvious how rich and complex are the perspectives opened up by this third book. But by trying to embrace too much, suggesting to some that he wanted to find the key to all of human history, didn't the author miss the mark and sacrifice the systematic quality of his work for the sake of an act of faith? Many of Girard's readers did not hide their bewilderment at these new horizons going well beyond the resolution of aporias introduced by Durkheim or Freud. In spite of very clear signs given from the beginning of his oeuvre, they refused to see that it was only *in a biblical light* that the sacrificial mechanism could have appeared. Girard didn't become a theologian. But there is an apocalyptic realism at the heart of his insight. There's the unfolding of a single tendency from the rise of undifferentiation in *Deceit, Desire, and the Novel* all the way to the "escalation to extremes" in *Battling to the End*. The resistance to this movement—its *katechon* in Pauline terms—can now no longer be offered by immanent mechanisms, but only, according to Girard, by the grace of the messianic event. From Saint Paul's perspective this event has been at work in and through time since the Resurrection: from the *chronos* of creation to the *eschaton* where time will be completed in eternity, this indefinite time stretches out, the Apostle says: it becomes this "time that remains" finally given as food for philosophical and theological thought.[3] For Girard, too, it's as if *historical* time had appeared ever since the Resurrection as a new object. "Violence," he often says, "is never lost to violence": henceforth, the impossibility of containing it *weighs* on human history. A return to the old order is less and less possible. The cause of this is now clear for Girard as it was for the first Christians; a new time has opened up and is now finally an object of thought.

The key thinker of messianic *kairos*, this mixture of time and eternity, is Saint Paul. Although he sharply critiqued the Letter to the Hebrews in *Things Hidden since the Foundation of the World*, before retracting his view on this key point and accepting the idea of a Christian sacrifice,[4] Girard had been constantly going back to Paul's letters ever since that time. To the point that to reformulate his hypotheses today, one must likewise go back to Saint Paul, who plays such a fundamental role in his theory. Indeed while reading Girard, one must make a constant effort to embrace the unity of his insight—a unity that is not without internal tension. From the beginning, Girard, who was trained as an archivist and historian, sensed that he was coming into contact with a *historical* object. Desire has a history, and the first book lays the foundations for it by describing—without being able to offer an underlying cause—the gradual rise of undifferentiation, the "ontological sickness" emerging from the erosion of all the old rituals. If Girard so strongly insisted on the idea that a certain history of desire came to a close with *In Search of Lost Time*, if, in his first articles in the 1950s, he clearly intuited the "end of the novel" while reading Saint-John Perse and Malraux, this was because he was still obscurely seeking what the Bible and the New Testament were going to bring him: a sense of urgency, and of the extreme gravity of certain choices.

So "the unity of triangular desire," structuring the shift from external to internal mediation and from admiration to rivalry, tightens the triangle and culminates in the logic of the duel. And Girard's final meditation on Clausewitz, where the escalation to extremes is seen as the dominant historical tendency, gives urgency to the idea of *an ultimate law* as the only alternative to catastrophe. But we shouldn't forget that the logic of Girard's thought—which deals with self-transcendence or with the immanent production of transcendence—has it that the rise of enslavement, the irreversible shift from one *mediation* to the other, is impossible to escape except *from within*. Such is the "intimate mediation" that we evoked together in *Battling to the End,*[5] a new type of mediation that can be thought of as imitation exceeding itself. Because it is a ritual logic, mimetic logic assumes this interiorization, this deepening of misrecognition into the "wisdom of love," to use Levinas's beautiful expression. This paradoxical imitation, or this rediscovered faith and trust in the other, takes the form of a conscious and deliberate identification with others.

Here we are getting at a profound dynamic within Girard's insight, which looks to find an immanent way of thinking about the shift from "external mediation" to "intimate mediation," from nature to grace, through the mimetic crisis of "internal mediation." External mediation bears within itself internal mediation, as the enlarged triangle bears within itself the smaller one right up until the point of undifferentiation where enemy brothers duel each other. Only an intimate mediation, the return to faith in a unique Mediator—the one whose Incarnation, for better or worse, has put divinity within reach—can save the religious structure and with it the long process of hominization. The return to external models is impossible, as Girard keeps saying, now that globalization is bringing about the erasure of all differences. And so a transcendence of imitation is necessary, a transcendence defined by the paradoxical imitation of Christ, which alone would make it possible to escape violent reciprocity. Messianic transcendence, the "God who comes to man," can be defined as the return *to* an authentic mediation, but also as the return *of* the one Mediator, the "resurrected victim" according to James Alison's precise and just expression.[6] This return to holiness in the heart of the catastrophe after the extremely slow deconstruction of all religious models, from the archaic sacred to the theologico-political sacred, is the same thing as the coming of the Kingdom, the likelihood of which increases at the same time as the "intelligence of the victim."[7]

At this stage, armed with the preceding analyses, we can give a new anthropological reading of the Resurrection: the Passion is a dynamic *repetition* of the religious structure, which is itself defined as a first repetition, the *sacrificial* victim repeating the *scapegoat* victim and reactivating the first trauma for cathartic ends (or as a vaccine against violence). This third form of repetition deepens awareness of the origin, working back to violent foundations. The "Christian resurrection" is thus nothing other than a repetition raised to the second power, already at work in time before the ultimate repetition—*parousia*—or, in more eschatological terms, before the return of the Messiah. In this context that return is nothing other than the advent of a humanity finally liberated from sacrificial religion. The innocent victim of the Bible repeats the *sacrificial* victim that already repeated the *scapegoat* victim; in a striking shortcut, the Resurrection resolves the enigma of the founding murder; the Passion, the event of the death and resurrection of the victim, is the ultimate variation on the religious structure. Girard's thought makes it possible to renew in decisive fashion the formulation of Christian dogma, giving it an "anthropo-theological" tenor that it was lacking. *The ultimate law, the one we must increasingly obey, is one and the same as messianic faith.* This faith in the absolute innocence of Christ pushes the structure beyond itself so to speak. And so we must turn to Saint Paul to understand the transcendence aimed at by Girard from the origin of his work. Faith's capacity for exceeding the law, a tension *both profoundly Jewish and profoundly Christian,* bringing together the best of both traditions just when they threaten to break apart for good, finds in Paul its exemplary thinker. Beyond the lively oppositions to his community of origin Saint Paul is the witness of a fundamental anthropological moment—that of a decisive transformation of religion, *much more than of a rupture* between Judaism and Christianity.

IV.

A Mimetic Approach to the Letter to the Romans

Girard never devoted a book specifically to Saint Paul. This fact in itself exculpates him from the preliminary analyses that follow, which implicate their author alone. Paul is nevertheless cited often enough in all of Girard's books (which, starting with *Things Hidden since the Foundation of the World*, are more or less all devoted to the apocalyptic effects of Judeo-Christian revelation) for a mimetic approach to the Letter to the Romans to be legitimately attempted. The density and depth of this text, its foundational character, and the fact that, for twenty or more years, it has been the object of a systematic investigation on the part of both theologians and philosophers, justifies examining some of its essential moments. What indeed does this text denounce if not a paradoxical impotence of Mosaic Law? It is as if, after the event of the Resurrection—the only event that has any meaning for Paul—the essential function of the Law necessitated a decisive confirmation *and* a decisive transformation. Here we're at the heart of a fundamental dialectic, the dialectic of typological interpretation, whose later excesses (due to Marcion) should not be imputed to Saint Paul.[1]

I will thus close the present study by going back over certain passages from the Letter to the Romans, which is a central text from the vantage point we have opened up. Here it is a question of the relationship between the Law and faith, Old and New Covenant. Prodded by judaizers who have come to tell the Galatians that only circumcision can give salvation, Paul retorts that it is by being attached to Christ *by faith* that we participate in the re-creation of a new humanity of which He is the prototype: in Girardian terms, a humanity that would no longer be threatened by mimetic rivalries. Paul must thus show that the Law leads to a dead end, for it is mysteriously bound up with sin. Here resides the Pauline scandal on which the Jews stumble in their refusal of the Christian interpretation of the relationship between faith and Law—a scandal that is also at the origin of Christian anti-Judaism's errors. Faced with this scandal, the exegetical explanations often compete to show that faith does not destroy the Law. They don't always give credence to the strange solidarity that Paul establishes between Law and sin. I would thus like to show what the mimetic hypothesis brings to our understanding of this primacy of "works" (i.e., the strict observance of ritual precepts) over the Law. But first let's reread an essential passage of the Letter (7:7–25):

> What then shall we say? That the law is sin? By no means! Yet, if it had not been for the law, I should not have known sin. I should not have known what it is to covet if the law had not said, "You shall not covet." But sin, finding opportunity in the commandment, wrought in me all kinds of covetousness. Apart from the law sin lies dead. I was once alive apart from the law, but when the commandment came, sin revived and I died; the very commandment which promised life proved to be death to me. For sin, finding opportunity in

the commandment, deceived me and by it killed me. So the law is holy, and the commandment is holy and just and good.

Did that which is good, then, bring death to me? By no means! It was sin, working death in me through what is good, in order that sin might be shown to be sin, and through the commandment might become sinful beyond measure. We know that the law is spiritual; but I am carnal, sold under sin. I do not understand my own actions. For I do not do what I want, but I do the very thing I hate. Now if I do what I do not want, I agree that the law is good. So then it is no longer I that do it, but sin which dwells within me. For I know that nothing good dwells within me, that is, in my flesh. I can will what is right, but I cannot do it. For I do not do the good I want, but the evil I do not want is what I do. Now if I do what I do not want, it is no longer I that do it, but sin which dwells within me. . . . Wretched man that I am! Who will deliver me from this body of death? Thanks be to God through Jesus Christ our

Lord! So then, I of myself serve the law of God with my mind, but with my flesh I serve the law of sin.

Saint Paul goes straight to the function of the Law here by emphasizing a single commandment: "You will not covet." What does this mean if not that the Law *is a decisive barricade against the danger of mimetic rivalry*? Whence the choice of the commandment that governs all the others. This commandment forbids "covetousness," which Girard in *Things Hidden* calls "appropriative mimesis." The intransitive dimension of the citation is fundamental. Mimetic logic is *the* danger par excellence, the fatal logic into which one must never enter. The Law seems thus to correspond to what Girard calls "external mediation" or "vertical transcendence" in his first book. But this external mediation, which should govern right conduct, guiding the subject, suddenly rises up to block him, becoming an obstacle and an "occasion of sin," which is paradoxical and even incomprehensible if the Law is divine, and if one considers that God is the external mediator par excellence. The subject, raised in the Law and guided by it, suddenly enters into rivalry with the commandment: "But sin, finding opportunity in the commandment, wrought in me all kinds of covetousness." The model has become a rival. This is a clear allusion to the garden of Eden, where the serpent's seduction insinuates the idea that the tree is desirable *because God desires it*.[2] I sin because I enter into rivalry with the Law. I am then acted upon by the "law of sin," this "other law at war with the law" (7:23). Veneration of the Law has become an obsession with the Law, and the benevolent God has become a jealous God who opposes my own will, blocking my way. We are no longer dealing with a transcendent God but with a God made from human hands, an idol.

"So then it is no longer I that do it," says Paul, "but sin which dwells within me": I am thus literally possessed by the "law of sin," which gives me a false representation of God (or the deceitful representation of a God who, by definition, eludes all representation). This demon that inhabits me, is a "deviated transcendence," Girard would say. It is this caricature, this counterfeit image of the Law that pushes me to do what I don't want to do, that "disorients" my desire, which was originally a desire for God, by offering mirages of a jealous divinity. We now understand the mechanism of this "deviated transcendence": to make of the commandment itself a rival is to transform transgression into self-divinization, because it means becoming the rival of God in person, as mimetic desire declares via the serpent's language in the Genesis narrative: "But the serpent said to the woman, 'You will not die. For God knows that when you eat of it your eyes will be opened, and you will be like God, knowing good and evil.'" (Genesis 3, 4–5). The variations of the triangle of desire, considered as so many stages of an "ontological sickness," have led us to understand that this divinization culminates in the death of the subject brought down by his own desire. Girard is here very close to the situation described by Saint Paul: "But sin, finding opportunity in the commandment, wrought in me all kinds of covetousness." When the external mediator becomes internal and when admiration is transformed into rivalry, when the model become too close is suddenly fetishized, the subject, obeying the law of desire, enters into a mimetic crisis that is one and the same as sin. Thus does the primacy of works over the Law bear witness to a paralysis of desire, which having been desire for God becomes desire to be God. The Mosaic Law, which could look like a healthy return to vertical transcendence, ends up being an "occasion of sin." A sinner is someone who thinks he can save himself, one who falls into the trap of denying a mediator who has become a rival, one who is possessed by the idol that he has made of God. It is because the Law is henceforth too close that I don't want to see it and that I transgress it.[3]

Scarcely has it been named and accorded a preeminent value, then, than the Law becomes an obstacle to the subject; it causes a fall into sin: "But sin, finding opportunity in the commandment, wrought in me all kinds of covetousness." What should have warded off covetousness provokes it. There is thus a constant shift from veneration of the Law of Moses to detestation of an "other law" that would have replaced it. Sin is from that point of view a lack of faith in the Law (for the Jews) and in Christ (for Christians). But why does the existence of the Law seem to call forth its transgression? We only half-understand the nature of this solidarity. The mystery begins to be cleared up, on the other hand, if we recall the "unity of triangular desire," that is to say the back-and-forth between the two kinds of mediation and the two types of relationship. The distant and unattainable model that I venerate and whose benefits I recognize starts to upset me as soon as it becomes too close and erupts into my life: a certain kind of veneration (the "other law") can lead to transgression; the loss of faith in the transcendence of God thus becomes an obsession with the Law. This obsession with the divine commandment is such that my only way of existing then consists in transgressing the Law.

Sin, which is, according to Girard, one and the same as mimetic desire, assumes a constant transition from a certain kind of veneration to the transgression of the Law, and from the Law transgressed to the Law venerated anew in a certain way. The mimetic subject, oscillating ceaselessly between these two poles, is riven, under a double subjection: to the Law of Moses by his "mind," and to the law of sin by his "flesh." Thus *the Pauline movement from the "law of reason" to the "law of flesh," and then from the "law of flesh" to the "law of reason," looks strangely like the movement we noted in the Girardian games of external and internal mediation, admiration and rivalry, "mimetic models" and "rational models."*[4] But what God are we speaking of here? Of the really and truly transcendent God whom I cannot name, or of the God that I picture and imagine as jealous? That is the whole question, and the definition of God as the external mediator par excellence begins to look wobbly. The back-and-forth from the rational to the mimetic, we have seen, occurs increasingly at the expense of the former, as if this link between the Law and sin testified in turn to a fatal exhaustion of rite. Faith then begins to appear as the only means of escaping this sinful logic. The Mosaic Law constitutes a progress in understanding of the mimetic mechanism, since it relates the prohibition to covetousness itself. But it no longer suffices as such *without the faith that is its foundation.*

This is why veneration can become fetishism or "primacy of works." It thus condemns us to sin, that is to say to servile revolt (which is anything but a redemption). True, the sinner always believes he can extricate himself from sin through a reiterated veneration of the Law: "So the law is holy, and the commandment is holy and just and good." But this impotent veneration inevitably reactivates sin. Here we encounter once again the mechanism of self-transcendence, which always "remakes" the spiritual out of the temporal. Only the spiritual lasts; the temporal falls back into the same old rut. Only the spiritual invents; the temporal endlessly repeats itself. It is thus necessary to consecrate the spiritual *as such*. This repetition is nothing other than the inbreaking of faith. The reappearance at the heart of the Law of that faith which founds it *creates a healthy distance with respect to the Law*; only this transcendence constitutes true proximity; only this transcendence makes possible authentic veneration. Life "according to the flesh" gives way to life "according to the spirit" (8:5–6). Such, according to Saint Paul, is the unprecedented event of the New Covenant that in no way contradicts the Old, but confirms and repeats it by going back, in some sense beyond the Mosaic Law, to Abrahamic faith: "I was once alive apart from the law"—creating a healthy distance with respect to a God that faith itself prevented from appearing, or from becoming an idol. True transcendence is beyond all representation. Should God enter the field of the visible, He will become an idol: "the Lord God walking in the garden in the cool of the day" (Genesis 3:8), seeking those who had just eaten of the forbidden fruit. The God of anger and punishment.

Thus faith does not suppress the Law; it "frees us from it," says Saint Paul, "delivers" us by suppressing a proximity that too often risks degenerating into promiscuity, which is to say into ritualism *and* into transgression. For that to happen, man had to be redeemed at the very point where he sinned, which is to say in the flesh: "For the law of the Spirit of life in Christ Jesus has set me free from the law of sin and death" (8:2). Completing the words of the prophets, the Incarnation of Christ fulfills the Law. Crowning the prophetic movement, Christ takes the place of the Law. Mediator of the Father, he pushes the latter back beyond all manifestation. And so we complete our exodus from sacrificial religion, an exodus of which the Law was a decisive stage. This stage is not however over, because it persists in the New Covenant. Called to imitate the Christic model, which repeats and incarnates the Law in a single gesture, the subject is liberated from the "law of the flesh." Imitating Christ, he no longer mindlessly trots out the Law, but instead deepens it: "I bear them witness that they have a zeal for God, but it is not enlightened. For, being ignorant of the righteousness that comes from God, and seeking to establish their own, they did not submit to God's righteousness. For Christ is the end of the law, that every one who has faith may be justified" (10:2–4). According to Saint Paul, it is thus the Incarnation of Christ that operates the unveiling of misrecognition, ridding us of the primacy of works and liberating humanity. The Christ, last prophet, Law made man, sharing the mortal condition without being afflicted by the "law of the flesh," is at once the *last law* and the *last victim*.

Such is the inflection that a mimetic analysis introduces into the interpretation of the Pauline text. The return of vertical transcendence now takes the form of the messianic *parousia*, that is to say of a growing *presence* of faith at the heart of the Law: God is no longer the external mediator par excellence, the one who dominates human history, but an intimate mediator, acting and revealing Himself at the heart of history. This presence no longer has anything in common with a veneration perpetually threatened by the fetishism potentially contained within it, due to the persistence of the "law of the flesh." It has nothing in common, either, with the threatening presence of the archaic sacred. Moreover it is as if the mimetic hypothesis were naturally present in a text where a veritable theology of imitation is elaborated: "For those whom he foreknew he also predestined to be conformed to the image of his Son, in order that he might be the first-born among many brethren" (8:29). As opposed to the instability of what Girard calls "mimetic models," "rational models" possess a stable nature. But the latter are increasingly susceptible to being transformed into their opposite. Only that faith which is capable of hearing The One Who Speaks in the Law makes it possible to avoid the perpetual ups and downs of mediation, for the emergence of this intimate model, "hidden since the foundation of the world," deals a fatal blow to the circle of sin. It is this intimate model whose insistent presence Paul felt within him in the question heard on the road to Damascus: "Why are you persecuting me?" Hence the doxology of the Letter, a liturgical finale that Girard enables us to better understand:

Now to him who is able to strengthen you
according to my gospel and the preachings of Jesus

Christ, according to the revelation of the mystery which was kept secret for long ages but is now disclosed and through the prophetic writings is made known to all nations, according to the command of the eternal God, to bring about the obedience of faith—to the only wise God be glory for evermore through Jesus Christ! Amen (16:25–27).

For this mimetic interpretation to become convincing, it remains to find in Paul's text the *sacrificial solution*. This will make it possible for us to understand what is at stake in transgression, that is to say the pure and simple suppression of the obstacle: first, *transgression* of the commandment, and then *sacrifice of the one who embodies it*, the Just One or the prophet who comes to reinvigorate the faith at the heart of the Law, the one who dares to speak in God's name or to let himself be called the "Son of God." If we find a trace of this victimary insight in the Pauline text, the causes of the paradoxical Law's impotence will be patent, and we will have located a mechanism that is valid for *all* human societies, including the Jewish society, which on this point does not constitute an exception. This mechanism is nothing other than the scapegoat mechanism at the origin of the emergence of rules and rituals. To see this one just has to follow out Paul's insight. Paul is trying to understand the "blindness" of his co-religionists, their inability to recognize the messianic *kairos*—in a word, their misrecognition. In his view, this inability comes from their obsession with the Law, which ends up making even obedience into an obstacle. And so we come to a second essential passage in the Letter, one where it is a question of the "stumbling stone" (9:30–33):

What shall we say, then? That Gentiles who did not pursue righteousness have attained it, that is, righteousness through faith; but that Israel who pursued the righteousness which is based on law did not succeed in fulfilling that law. Why? Because they did not pursue it through faith, but as if it were based on works. They have stumbled over the stumbling stone, as it is written,

"Behold, I am laying in Zion a stone that will make men stumble, a rock that will make them fall;

and he who believes in him will not be put to shame."

The fact of having privileged "works," that is to say a literal interpretation of the Law and a certain type of veneration, made the "Jews according to the flesh"[5] blind to the foundation stone announced by Isaiah. It rendered them deaf to the voice that speaks in the Law. It is this "unenlightened zeal," this aggravated misrecognition, that made them reject the Just One. In Saint Paul's mind, then, there are two ways of reading this "stumbling stone." It is because they have fetishized the Law that it has become an obstacle with which they collide, an "occasion of sin." And it is this mindless repetition of the letter, this blind ritualism, that has made them deaf to the prophets. The latter, who denounced their blindness, have thus in turn become a *scandal*, a "stumbling stone," an obstacle *that must be eliminated*. Lacking faith, the "Jews according to the flesh" have had nothing but "works," that is to say a formalism, a terrified obsession with the Law. This sacralized Law, calling forth its own transgression, is exceeded by the prophets who speak in its name. Among the prophets, the messianic word resonated already, alerting against the law of the flesh, that "law at war with the law" (7:23). It was thus logical that Jesus should in turn be subjected to the fate of the prophets, and that his blasphemous insistence should result in his undergoing the fate of criminals. The blindness of the "Jews according to the flesh" thus goes beyond Israel and is valid for *all* peoples. *All* peoples "according to the flesh" have immolated innocent victims: lynching or lapidation makes the rite (observance of the Law) regress to the scapegoat mechanism, even when it is a matter of an authorized punishment. The fetishism of the Law is then inscribed in the wake of sacrifices; it is logical that those who retain only the letter of the Law should exclude or sacrifice those who remind them of its spirit. The faith restores to the Law its transcendence, preventing it from becoming once again an "occasion of sin." It liberates humanity from the law of flesh that prevents it from obeying the Law. It is in this sense only that one can say that Christ fulfills the Law: Word made flesh, he fulfills it in the sense that he *makes himself heard* in it once and for all. The sinner is the one who refuses to hear the One who speaks in the

Law.[6] This God who speaks in the Law is not a God looking down on the world (an external mediator who might always become an internal mediator, provoking sin), but an intimate mediator, a God who is only fully transcendent because he resides in the heart of everyone.

Re-reading the Letter to the Romans through the prism of the mimetic hypothesis brings to light at last *what should be* the relationship between Christians and Jews, an eschatological relationship, one that is alone capable of bringing forth the "new heaven" and the "new earth." This isn't simply a matter of a mere appropriative mimesis or of a mere metaphysical desire (which is the desire to steal from the other his very being, even if the theme of "*Verus Israel*" is indeed inspired by this unwarranted interpretation), but of a rivalry or of a zeal *in faith*, that is to say of an emulation. It is because this emulation henceforth exists between Jewish ritual and Christian ritual that humanity is given an opportunity to go beyond mindless ritual repetition, mere habit, decrepitude— and *to hear the Word*. What does this mean except that the two Covenants are now but one in messianic time, the "time [that] has grown very short" (1 Corinthians 7:29), an instant in which past and present contract? It is striking to see that the driving force of this temporal synthesis is defined by Paul in explicitly mimetic terms. This brings us to another decisive passage in the Letter to the Romans (11:11–15; my emphasis):

So I ask, have they stumbled so as to fall? By no means! But through their trespass salvation has come to the Gentiles, *so as to make Israel jealous.* Now if their trespass means riches for the world, and if their failure means riches for the Gentiles, how much more will their full inclusion mean!

Now I am speaking to you Gentiles. Inasmuch then as I am an apostle to the Gentiles, I magnify my ministry in order to make my fellow Jews jealous, and thus save some of them. For if their rejection means the reconciliation of the world, what will their acceptance mean but life from the dead?

Faith in the One who speaks in the Law makes it possible to transcend the law of the flesh. And this faithfulness sends the law of the flesh into a fury. It obviously cannot be denied that here it is the victim who escaped several stonings who speaks, the one who knows exactly what the "*droit tumultuaire*" (or "right of the crowd")[7] of the antique world is all about, right by which the sovereign crowd decides who is or is not guilty. But at the same time there is another way of understanding this "jealousy of Israel," one that is much more dynamic and much less sacrificial, and above all much better equipped to avoid trotting out the same old clichés about Paul's alleged antisemitism. The movement toward the pagans is "reconciliation of the world"; the reintegration of Israel is "resurrection of the dead," marking the end of the separation (enacted by the Law) between Jews and pagans. The reconciliation of pagans and Christians is a prelude to the resurrection of the dead that is literally the return of Israel (and toward Israel), which seems to be one and the same as the *parousia*. It is thus quite deliberately that Paul wants to "excite the jealousy" of the "Jews according to the flesh," that he wants to force them to become "Jews according to the spirit," to leave their obsessive-compulsive repetition behind so that they repeat the Word, identify with the One who speaks in the Law, imitate the Just One, become "Sons of God." In this sense, the Suffering Servant in Isaiah is less a foreshadowing of Christ than he is himself already the Messiah, and the "enlightened zeal" of Israel spares Christians from all idolatry of the Christic model, warning them in their turn against all bad imitation, the dangers of mindless repetition. We thus cannot stray from the idea that apart from the polemical weight of such an argument, there comes to the surface here a very new idea against which many of the blind have butted up against in their turn—that of the Judeo-Christian emulation which punctuates messianic time. It may even be in this tension proper to Judeo-Christian revelation that the dynamic of religious structure is played out.

But if Paul's Jewish contemporaries were deaf to the voice of the One who speaks in the Law, what about those who made those same Jews into the scapegoats of their own blindness? We know how much blood and ink has been spilled over the theme of "*Verus Israel.*" On this point, we cannot turn away from the terrible question of a Jacob Taubes: "I raise the question of the political potentials contained within theological metaphors."[8] When, with

Girard, one is alerted to the dangers of all unanimity, it is easy to spot that of a literal reading of the phrase I have just cited above: "their rejection means the reconciliation of the world." Nevertheless we must not impute to Saint Paul the responsibility for these horrors, even if it is undeniable that his anti-legalism (this latent intermingling in his writings of the Law of Moses and the law of the flesh) served the excesses of Christian anti-Judaism. But more stimulating by far is the method that aims, through a rereading of the finale of the Letter, to better understand the nature of the dynamic emulation between Jews and Christians. The *sacramental* logic preached by the Apostle is clearly a form of *displaced sacrifice*. This is yet another proof—if another one is needed—of why it is worth reading this Letter in light of the Girardian hypothesis: if, for example, there are still traces of bloody sacrifice in circumcision, there are no longer any at all in baptism. This is what Paul means when he speaks of an excess of the Law in faith. But on the other hand, the persistence of Jewish ritual at a time when (as Lucien Scubla has noted)[9] the meaning of Christian ritual is crumbling, proves two things: the fundamental character of ritual in the maintenance of a tradition, and the vital necessity for Christians of coming back to their Jewish source. This is the reason why in Saint Paul's mind baptism must compete in effectiveness with circumcision. Did Christians manage to do this? The risks that secularization poses to the conscience of the West—risks which at every turning underline by contrast the insistent fidelity of the Jewish people—sometimes make one wonder.

Conclusion

Throughout this essay we have been seeking to grasp the essential difference between mindless and mindful repetition, slavish copy and faithful imitation. Girard tells us that misrecognition is what structures ritual. But let's not rid ourselves too quickly of this obscure misrecognition, in the name of a supposed lucidity given to us by reason. For it is always in ritual practice, or rather in the awareness inherent to this practice, that the wisdom of religion is given. It is because they will compete against each other, Saint Paul says, that Jews and Christians will *together* leave behind the law of the flesh and become "beings according to the spirit." It is through this emulation that "life from the dead" will take place. That is why Girard constantly denounces the misrecognition proper to modern reason. We must be attentive to the voice that speaks in the Law, repeating not the letter but the spirit. This plea is not sectarian. It seeks to be faithful to what Sylvain Lévi, the specialist of Vedic India at the end of the nineteenth century, called a "ritology," that is to say an internal understanding of rite, an understanding that is one with repetition understood as *an open rather than a closed imitation*, as intelligence of ritual, in both senses of the genitive. It is because in Girard's mind Christian revelation is the most radical advance that was made in the deepening of this awareness, in this repetition of religious structure, that we must attempt to understand the revolution that it accomplishes. Christianity speaks the truth of religion, but it does not do away with religion: it confirms and transforms it.

Of course, we might regret that Girard never sought to construct a theory of Christian ritual. Ecumenical reasons discouraged him from undertaking this task. But nonetheless his work bears within itself powerful reflections on repetition. It makes of him a key contemporary of postwar French thought (Levinas, Derrida, Deleuze . . .) which in his own way he helped to make known in America. If repetition is indeed the modality of thought that connects it to its religious origin,[1] then Girard is also a philosopher, even if the concepts he deploys sometimes deserve clarification, so sweeping are they. What remains is a very strong insight, which infuses his whole oeuvre: the more we "know what we are doing," the less efficacious is ritual, while at the same time the responsibility that befalls us grows ever greater and even becomes unbearable. So we come back to the lesson of *Deceit, Desire, and the Novel*, in which Girard highlights the extent to which blindness increases at the same time as lucidity: it is the narrator's father, the most snobbish inhabitant of Combray, who spots and understands Legrandin's snobbery. Just as the coquette's desire increases at the same time as the desire of those who pursue her, so too does blindness grow along with lucidity. It is this lesson that the various sorts of "Marcionists" refuse to hear, for they refuse the continuity of the two Covenants. The anti-ritualist does not realize the degree to which his apparent surplus of lucidity blinds him still more than it enlightens him. The more I will have an intellectual grasp of ritual, to the point of thinking I can do without it, the more I risk "forgetting founding violence," as Girard says at the end of *Violence and the Sacred*, thus exposing myself to the return of "essential violence." The ruse of religion consists in forcing itself onto our memory just when we thought we had left it behind. Accepting the fact that there has been a "failure" of historical Christianity,[2] or that politics has seriously misunderstood the prophetic, does not prevent us from hoping for a possible fulfillment of the slow process of hominization. But only on condition, Girard affirms, that we take the structure of religion into account, and recognize that man is the fruit of sacrifice, and that to forget this is to expose ourselves to the worst kind of waywardness. To think about religion as that which we must always *repeat*, always deepen, and not as that which must be surpassed once and for all—this would be to have taken a crucial step.

Girard placed his bets on the existence of an essential *difference*, which could be called prophetic or messianic. Contrary to what some of his critics have too hastily affirmed,[3] there is no misappropriation of Judaism by Christianity here, but rather an attempt to grasp the dynamic structure of religion itself. It is in the ritual emulation immanent to the Christian "rupture" that another transcendence is made present at the heart of history. The intimate bond that both links and opposes Jewish and Christian traditions speaks not only in favor of a differentiated permanence of religious structure but also for the definitive shift enacted within this structure. It is thus that we will succeed in thinking through the identity *and* the difference of these two traditions. The Girardian conception of Judeo-Christianity does not presuppose that a reconciliation has been effected between the two traditions—the very idea is suspect, and assumes an absorption of the biblical into the Christian. Quite to the contrary, it is in a positive state of conflict that we might succeed in bringing intellectual clarity to this essential dialogue: the "jealousy" that Paul wants to trigger among his Jewish brothers will become an essential motor and not a static reappropriation of Jewish heritage—the motor of a history that Paul senses has not yet come to a close.

Prior to any trinitarian theology where the divinization *and* the hominization proper to Christian experience are defined, *this* is the essential catholicity that can be extracted from Girard's oeuvre, and which was already indicated by the discreet emblem of the "finger of God" of the Combray belfry—an unceasingly reaffirmed compossibility between Jews and Christians, on the one hand, and between Jews and pagans on the other. Having gone out toward the pagans because of Israel's refusal, the arrow of the promise comes back toward Israel. The "justification" of archaic religion through revelation of the innocent victim in the Bible, which alone "reconciles," that is to say gives a complete understanding of the religious phenomenon, brings the pagans back toward Israel, at the same time as it brings Israel toward the pagans. There is no valid identitarian election, or else one falls back into an *exclusive* conception of religion. From this point of view, election can only be operational, and mimetic anthropology enables us to better grasp the meaning of Pauline catholicity. *All* peoples are called to election. Christian revelation reveals the profound unity of religious structure, whether pagan or Jewish. When this structure is understood in a dynamic fashion, religion—far from being obscurantism or ritualism—will be grasped as the motor of hominization. In this way, Girard's thought could help us to better understand messianic hope, and what constitutes its difference with respect to other forms of religion. When the "Jews according to the flesh," who in spite of their refusal remain fundamentally in a state of election (thus the essential character of persistent circumcision), will have become "Jews according to the spirit," and conversely when the "non-Jews according to the flesh" will have become "non-Jews according to the spirit," when Jews and pagans will have set aside the law of the flesh, then the two covenants will be but one, and the tension proper to messianism will be resolved. The scapegoat mechanism will have drawn its final breath. The believer will conclude that hominization has been completed, and man divinized at last; the skeptic (or the enlightened unbeliever) will wonder if man himself has disappeared along with the gods. All bets are on.

Notes

Introduction

1. René Girard, *Battling to the End: Conversations with Benoît Chantre* (East Lansing: Michigan State University Press, 2009).

2. Girard, *Battling to the End,* chapters 6 and 7. We will refer in particular to chapter 6, where Girard reveals the cardinal importance of Hölderlin in the formation of his anthropological insight: "The plan [that of a 'new mythology'] faded, and in the end only Hölderlin continued it, but in a work that was broken and fragmented, and finally contradicted every didactic aspect that Hegel and Schelling had wanted to include. It takes the form of a central intuition based on the observation that there is absolute similarity but also absolute difference between the Christian and the archaic. . . . The 'monotheism of reason and the heart,' which in fact

means Catholicism, is the only way to rediscover a degree of stability in an equilibrium that has become essentially unstable, *a situation that is a result of the Revelation.* Everything is adrift, extremely fragile. . . . When he argues this, the poet is no longer under the influence of his friends. He is seeking less a synthesis than a kind of compossibility between the archaic and the Christian. He is well aware that *both a difference and a similarity have to be taken into account*, and that the Greek religion cannot be used as a weapon against Christianity. Christianity has changed the Greek religion forever. . . . Despite the pressure he suffers from fashion and friends, the poet feels the truth: Dionysus is violence and Christ is peace. I cannot think of a better way of putting what we are trying to say. It is said by a Christian whose rare utterances during the time of his retreat include the statement 'I am precisely on the point of becoming Catholic.' This anecdote interests me in that it provides an anthropological basis for Catholic *stability*, which is the only thing that can hold the world together after the shock of the Revelation. However, we have to be careful not to portray Hölderlin as too Christian. His nature was deeply mystical; that cannot be denied. But we also cannot deny that his Protestantism and piety closed the way for him to Catholic cheerfulness" (p. 126–130). This insight will be reprised in chapter 7 with regard to Germaine de Staël and Charles Baudelaire.

I. From Vertical Transcendence to Deviated Transcendence

1. René Girard, *Deceit, Desire, and the Novel*, trans. Yvonne Freccero (Baltimore: Johns Hopkins University Press, 1965), 214.

2. Girard, *Deceit*, 215. This point is essential: external mediation (the imitation of the desire of a distant model) is always potentially an internal mediation (the imitation of the desire of a model who is too close); it is thus a *contained* pathology: "The opposition between *external* and *internal* mediation is not an opposition between Good and Evil, it is not an absolute separation. A closer examination of Combray will reveal, in a nascent state, all the features of the worldly salons" (Girard, *Deceit*, 213–214). The only difference between the two worlds is thus *the loss of spontaneous faith in our models*.

3. Marcel Proust, *In Search of Lost Time*, vol. 1, *Swann's Way*, trans. C.K. Scott Moncrieff, revised by Terence Kilmartin and D.J. Enright (Modern Library, 1992), 90–91.

4. Marcel Proust, *Time Regained*, trans. Andreas Mayor and Terence Kilmartin, revised by D.J. Enright (Modern Library, 1999), 264.

5. Girard, *Deceit*, 215.

6. I will refer especially to chapter 3 of *Deceit, Desire, and the Novel*, "The Metamorphoses of Desire."

7. Girard, *Deceit*, 141.

8. Girard, *Deceit*, 141.

9. Girard radicalizes Hegel: it is literally by *panicking* the master-slave dialectic, *by making the mimetic relationship that is both asymmetrical* (pitting a master against a slave) *and reciprocal* (each being both master and slave to the other) that Girard—through the variations of triangular desire—conceptualizes a growing slavery to the other understood as a fascinating model who increasingly becomes an obstacle standing in the disciple's path, but *who also becomes ever more an obstacle to himself.* This is a crucial point. The reciprocity of the mimetic relationship (which Girard calls "double mediation") makes it so that

the other cannot alienate himself with respect to me unless I am myself "alienated with respect to myself," my own slave, as it were. Thus the paradoxes of the "coquette" or the "indifferent woman," who appear to be the victors in the game of desire but are in fact paradoxical heroes of an "asceticism in the service of desire." Desire does not grow on one side while diminishing on the other (this would be the quantitative conception of *libido*); it grows, writes Girard, "on both sides at once" (see the preface to René Girard, *La Conversion de l'art*, Carnets Nord, 2008). The three poles of the triangle—the subject mad with love, the coquette loving herself, and the object of their common love—have tipped into the imaginary.

10. "As the role of the *metaphysical* grows greater in desire, that of the *physical* diminishes in importance. As the mediator draws near, passion becomes more intense and the object is emptied of concrete value" (Girard, *Deceit*, 85).

11. In *Battling to the End*, Girard takes this "aggravation of ontological sickness" a step further, evoking—along the lines of Dostoevskian "possession"—the figure of the terrorist. He points out the simultaneous emergence at the time of the Spanish war in 1808 of regular and irregular

armies. The "populace in arms" is both Napoleon's strength and that of the guerrillas who are fighting against him. The broadening of armed conflicts goes hand in hand with the *exacerbated individualism* of the partisans and later of terrorists. Which shows that it is indeed the asymmetry and reciprocity of modern conflicts (in a word, their mimetic nature) that makes it possible to define them as wars of *ressentiment*.

12. "Don Quixote has surrendered to Amadis the individual's fundamental prerogative: he no longer chooses the objects of his own desire—Amadis must choose for him. The disciple pursues objects which are determined for him, or at least seem to be determined for him, by the model of all chivalry. We shall call this model the *mediator* of desire. Chivalric existence is the *imitation* of Amadis in the same sense that the Christian's existence is the imitation of Christ." (Girard, *Deceit*, 1–2). Triangular desire is thus a figure of Christian desire. "In Cervantes the mediator is enthroned in an inaccessible heaven and transmits to his faithful follower a little of his serenity. In Stendhal, this same mediator has come down to earth. The clear distinction between these two types of relationship

between mediator and subject indicates the enormous spiritual gap which separates Don Quixote from the most despicably vain of Stendhal's characters" (Girard, *Deceit*, 8). Thus we never desire autonomously: in former times our respect for models attested to this. But inasmuch as those models were one and the same as culture in general, this truth scandalized nobody. It was Christian revelation, Girard suggests from the outset, that made this truth scandalous: Christ come down to earth puts divinity "in arm's reach." *Should faith in the transcendence of the One Mediator be lacking*, men will become "gods in the eyes of each other."

13. Girard, *Deceit*, 103–104.

14. The second paragraph of *Deceit, Desire, and the Novel* ("We shall call this model the *mediator* of desire. Chivalric existence is the *imitation* of Amadis in the same sense that the Christian's existence is the imitation of Christ") should be brought into proximity with a passage from the first chapter of Max Scheler's *Ressentiment*: "Each of us—noble or common, good or evil—continually compares his own value with that of others. If I choose a model, a 'hero,' I am somehow tied to such a comparison. All jealousy, all

ambition, and even an ideal like the 'imitation of Christ' is full of such comparisons." Max Scheler, *Ressentiment*, ed. Lewis A. Coser, trans. William W. Holdheim (New York: Schocken Books, 1961), 53. It is very interesting to note that these two critiques of the Nietzschean analysis of ressentiment see the Christian model as an alternative to the dangers of comparisons that curdle into ressentiment, and ressentiment as a caricature of the imitation of Christ.

II. Self-Transcendence, the Scapegoat Mechanism, and the Institution of Sacrifice

1. Lucien Scubla, "René Girard et la renaissance de l'anthropologie religieuse," in *René Girard*, ed. Mark R. Anspach (Paris: Cahiers de L'Herne, 2008), 105–109.

2. René Girard, *Violence and the Sacred*, trans. Patrick Gregory (Baltimore: Johns Hopkins University Press, 1977), 309.

3. René Girard, *Sacrifice*, trans. Matthew Patillo and David Dawson (East Lansing: Michigan State University Press, 2011).

4. It should be noted that Girard intuits this phenomenon

of convergence in his first book, where the indifferent dandy or coquette, practicing an "asceticism for the sake of desire," capturing others' desire by worshipping him or herself, draws more and more individuals into worship that becomes collective, and of which the indifferent character himself eventually becomes the scapegoat: unable to obtain a lasting triumph over the crowd of the "possessed," Stavrogin ends up committing suicide, interiorizing within his split subjectivity the social opprobrium directed at him.

5. See Georges Hubert de Radkowski's article, "La première théorie athée du religieux" (*Le Monde*, 27 October 1972), published upon the release of *Violence and the Sacred* and cowritten with Girard, as the latter reveals in "La Violence et le sacré," the filmed interviews directed by Pierre-André Boutang, Annie Chevalley, and myself (Éditions Montparnasse, 2006, DVD).

6. The sacrificial victim is the first thing substituted *in place of* something else—the first symbol. See René Girard, with Pierpaolo Antonello and João Cezar de Castro Rocha, *Evolution and Conversion: Dialogues on the Origin of Culture* (New York: Bloomsbury, 2008), chapter 4.

7. Girard, *Violence and the Sacred*, 318.

8. Paul Dumouchel, *The Barren Sacrifice: An Essay on Political Violence*, trans. Mary Baker (East Lansing: Michigan State University Press, 2015).

9. John 11:50, quotes from the Old and New Testaments throughout from *The Ignatius Bible: Revised Standard Version; Second Catholic Edition* (San Francisco: Ignatius Press, 2006).

10. Cf. certain pages in *Violence and the Sacred*: "Religious beliefs are compromised by the decadent state of ritual. . . . The difference between blood spilt for ritual and for criminal purposes no longer holds. The Heraclitus fragment appears in even sharper relief when compared to analogous passages in the Old Testament. The preexilian prophets Amos, Isaiah, and Micah denounce in vehement terms the impotence of the sacrificial process and ritual in general. *In the most explicit manner they link the decay of religious practices to the deterioration of contemporary behavior. Inevitably, the eroding of the sacrificial system seems to result in the emergence of reciprocal violence.* Neighbors who had previously discharged their mutual aggression on a third party, joining together in the sacrifice of an 'outside' victim, now turn to sacrificing one another" (Girard,

Violence and the Sacred, 43; my emphasis). Here it can be seen that the loss of faith in the other and the loss of faith in ritual are for Girard one and the same thing. This defiance divinizes the other and at the same time makes him into an obstacle. Faith regained, on the other hand, reopens a communion between the other and self.

11. Here I am following Girard, who (wrongly, in some sense) does not consider the essay on Dostoyevsky as a second book in its own right. In fact, Girard's first three major books correspond to the three great acts of his thought: triangular desire, the scapegoat mechanism, and Judeo-Christian revelation.

III. Messianic Transcendence

1. René Girard, *Things Hidden since the Foundation of the World: Research Undertaken in Collaboration with Jean-Michel Oughourlian and Guy Lefort*, trans. Stephen Bann and Michael Metteer (Stanford, CA: Stanford University Press, 1987).

2. Marcion, a heresiarch excommunicated in Rome in 144, is known thanks to his Christian opponents (Tertullian,

Theophilus of Antioch) as holding to a radical Pauline position, retaining from Scripture only the Gospel of Luke and Paul's ten Letters. "Marcionism" designates more generally a tendency to reject the continuity between Old and New Testaments, on the pretext that they refer to different Gods.

3. For all of these questions relating to messianism, we will refer to Giorgio Agamben's essay *The Time That Remains: A Commentary on the Letter to the Romans*, trans. Patricia Daley (Stanford, CA: Stanford University Press, 2005).

4. See Girard, *The One by Whom Scandal Comes*, trans. M. B. DeBevoise (East Lansing: Michigan State University Press, 2014), and in particular the article "Mimetic Theory and Theology." To accept the idea of a Christian sacrifice was indeed to abandon the illusory position of anti-sacrificial superiority that Girard believed he had found in *Things Hidden since the Foundation of the World*. Self-sacrifice defines biblical religion against archaic religion, and puts Girard's thought back into the framework of what could be called a "martyrial" anthropology: the death of any innocent makes the possibility of the Kingdom more concrete. A systematic confrontation with the thought of

Emmanuel Levinas—Girard's contemporary—would make it possible to leave behind aspects of this "self-sacrifice" that are still too sacrificial, so as to define an "allowing oneself be sacrificed" that places all responsibility for violence on the executioners' shoulders.

5. Girard, *Battling to the End*, 158–169.

6. James Alison, *The Joy of Being Wrong: Original Sin through Easter Eyes* (New York: The Crossroad, 1998). To speak of the "resurrected victim" rather than of the "resurrected Christ" makes it possible to think about the Easter event in a fresh light, conceiving it less as a "classic" religious resurrection, which would eliminate Christian difference in the vise grip of a general religious theory, than as Easter revelation, a resurrection of a new type introduced by Christian *repetition* in the history of religions. One could then define the "resurrection of the victim" (both the victim's sacrifice and the revelation of his innocence) as a last repetition of religious structure, a comprehensive repetition that confers on the structure its dynamic nature, confirming the archaic and in the same gesture transforming it.

7. Alison, *The Joy of Being Wrong*.

IV. A Mimetic Approach to the Letter to the Romans

1. Recall that the typological method consists in linking
    the Hebrew Bible to the New Testament, this in the key
    of a *figural* anticipation (or expectation): certain biblical
    "types" figure Christian "anti-types." The manna given
    to the Hebrews in the desert *prefigures* the Eucharist, the
    "suffering servant" in Isaiah *announces* Christ, etc. The
    temporal synthesis between a moment of the biblical
    past and a moment of the messianic present tears the
    one who operates this synthesis from the slavery of time:
    this synthesis is the prelude to the eruption of *kairos*
    as an instant of eternity. This bedazzlement is the only
    hint, the only "foretaste" of authentic transcendence—a
    transcendence that, strictly speaking, is no longer "vertical"
    because it is inscribed in the compressed horizontality of
    history. In certain ways, Proust has a comparable experience
    in *Time Regained*, whence the importance of "novelistic
    revelation" in Girard's first insight.

2. See Jean-Michel Oughourlian, *The Genesis of Desire*, trans.
    Eugene Webb (East Lansing: Michigan State University
    Press, 2010), chapter 2, "The Creation and the Fall."

3. Cf. the commentary in the French *"Traduction oecuménique de la Bible"* (TOB) (Charols, France: Cerf-SBF, 1988 and 2004), to which Girard often referred: "At issue here is sinful humanity not yet justified by faith. . . . We must be on our guard against making the conflict described in verses 15–24 a psychological analysis or the description of a personal analysis of Paul himself. The passage levels a gaze on sinful humanity that only the light of faith has made possible. Only faith reveals and manifests in the life of man enslaved to sin certain aspects whose meaning he could not have discovered on his own. Paul's thought could be transcribed pretty exactly in terms of *alienation* (in the deepest sense of the word as suggested by its etymology— belonging to another). Sin alienates man in the sense that it involves him in a destiny that contradicts his deepest aspirations and the vocation to which God is calling him."

4. Cf. *Battling to the End*, op. cit.

5. Here I am using Giorgio Agamben's terminology in his commentary on the Letter to the Romans, *The Time that Remains*, op. cit., p. 49–52, namely "Jews according to the flesh" and "Jews according to the breath," "non-Jews according to the flesh," and "non-Jews according to the

breath." This terminology comes from an interpretation of the Pauline theory of the "remnant of Israel" according to which this "remnant" is constituted by the fact of being "according to the breath" and not "according to the flesh." Thus "messianic beings" (the expression chosen by Agamben instead of "Christians" or "Judeo-Christians") include Jews and non-Jews, "Jews according to the breath" and "non-Jews according to the breath." In logical terms, the "messianic beings" are "non-non-Jews" (neither Jews nor pagans). This "division of the division," to use Agamben's expression, is the division created by faith within the division created by the Law; a division to the second power, it neutralizes the first and renders it null and void. It thus liberates the "remnant of Israel." This division of the division, which defines faith, bears some resemblance to that which, in the framework of Girard's anthropology of sacrifice, could be called the sacrifice of sacrifice, which reveals the victim's innocence.

6. See François Euvé, *Crainte et tremblement. Une histoire du péché* (Paris: Seuil, 2010).

7. The "right of the crowd" is the legal framework within which the Romans occupying Palestine inscribed the

stoning ritual authorized in Leviticus. See Marie-Françoise Baslez, *Saint Paul, artisan d'un monde chrétien* (Paris: Fayard, 2008).

8.   Jacob Taubès, *La Théologie politique de Paul*, (Paris: Seuil and Traces Écrites, 2006), p. 105. Cf. also Jean-Michel Rey, *Paul ou les ambiguïtés* (Paris: Éditions de l'Olivier, 2008).

9.   Lucien Scubla, "Le sacrifice protège les hommes de la violence. Un apport de René Girard à l'anthropologie du sacrifice," *Raison présente*, no. 170 (2009): 103–116.

Conclusion

1.   See Vincent Delecroix's preface to Sigmund Freud, *Religion*, trans. Denis Messier (Paris: Gallimard, 2012).

2.   Girard, *Battling to the End*, op. cit.

3.   Cf. for example Shmuel Trigano, *L'E(xc)lu, entre juifs et chrétiens* (Paris: Denoël, 2002), in which Girard is accused of "laudatory appropriation" with regard to Israel.